# Techniques

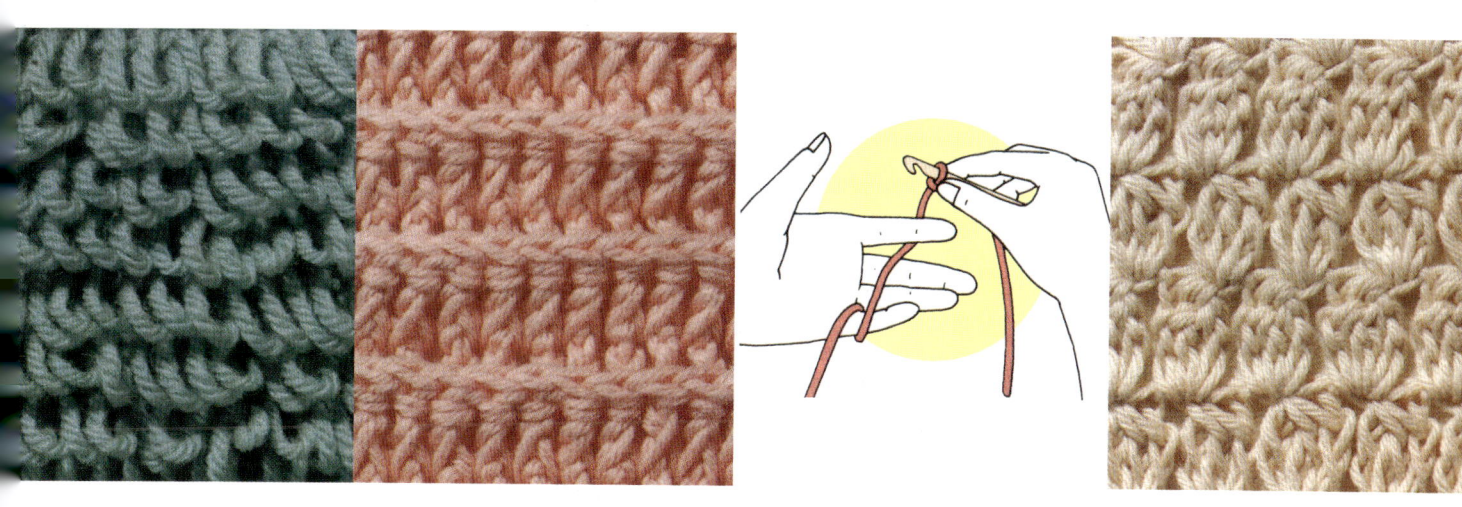

# Reader's Digest

The Reader's Digest Association, Inc.
Pleasantville, NY/Montreal/Sydney

# Contents

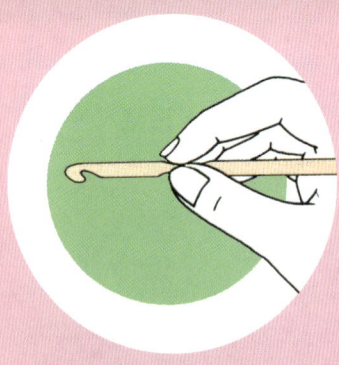

*Holding the hook—Page 10*

*Half-double crochet—Page 14*

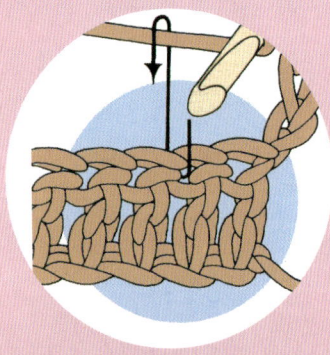

*Working in rows —Page 18*

**4**  INTRODUCTION

**6**  THE BASICS
About your kit 7

**8**  HOOKS AND YARNS
Hooks 8
Yarns 9
Substituting yarns 9

**10**  GETTING STARTED
Holding the hook 10
Controlling the yarn 10

**11**  FOUNDATION CHAINS
Making a slip loop 11
Making chain stitches (ch) 11

**12**  BASIC STITCHES
Slip stitch (ss) 12
Single crochet (sc) 13
Half-double crochet (hdc) 14
Double crochet (dc) 15
Triple crochet (tr) 16
Double-triple crochet (dtr) 17

**18**  MAKING A FLAT FABRIC
Working in rows 18

**19**  SHAPING
Single increases 19
Multiple increases 20
Single decreases 21
Double decreases 22
Multiple decreases 23

**24    WORKING IN ROUNDS**

**26    COLOR EFFECTS**
Joining in new yarn at the end of a row 26
Changing color in the middle of a row 27
Working stripes 27
Jacquard designs 28
Carrying yarn across back of work 28
Weaving in yarn 28
Working from a color chart 29

**30    STITCH VARIATIONS**
Raised stitches 30
Raised double crochet at the back 30
Raised double crochet at the front 31
Ridged effects 31
Loops 32
Clusters 32
Soft clusters 33
Bobble stitch 33

**34    FILET CROCHET**
Basic grid background 34
Using charts for filet crochet designs 35
Shaping filet crochet 36
Increasing a space at the start of a row 36
Decreasing a space at the start of a row 36
Decreasing a space at the end of a row 36
Variations on mesh backgrounds 37
Chain overlays 37
Woven overlays 37

**38    CHARTED STITCHES**
Shorthand symbols 38
Charted motif 39

**40    INDEX**

*Working in rounds—Page 24*

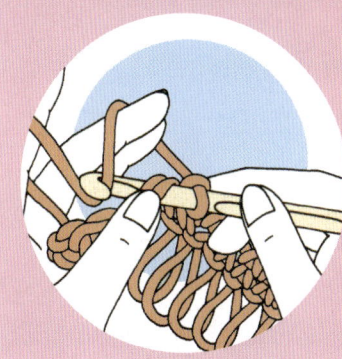
*Loop stitches—Page 32*

*Charted stitches—Page 39*

# Introduction

Most forms of craft can be dated to a certain place and time, thanks to archaeological and pictorial evidence, but no one is quite sure when and where crochet got its start. What is certain, though, is that it has evolved into a popular modern handicraft, worthy of a place alongside knitting and embroidery.

Irish crochet rose

## EARLY ORIGINS

Although few examples survive, evidence suggests that crochet was around in parts of Europe as early as the 15th and 16th centuries, when it was called nun's work or nun's lace.

Crochet became popular with women all over Europe in the 1800s, thanks to the dedicated efforts of a Frenchwoman, Mlle. Riego de la Branchardiere, who took old-style designs for needle and bobbin lace and published them as crochet patterns that could easily be stitched. However, these early patterns are very vague, often with large portions of the instructions missing, and were more useful for passing down patterns from mother to daughter than fully recording them—a far cry from the accurate and precise crochet patterns of today.

## A COTTAGE INDUSTRY

By the mid-1800s crochet had spread through Europe and reached Ireland, where it was, literally, a lifesaver. Irish crochet, or guipure lace, was introduced to Ireland by Irish nuns trained in a convent in France, and what started as a cottage industry soon became a way for women to supplement their income and support their families during the great potato famine. Women worked in small groups, and it was common practice for each person to specialize in making one element of a design, whether it was a flower or a leaf, and for another "finisher" to put the whole thing together—very similar

*Shawls have always been popular crochet projects. Instructions for this beautiful Cobweb Shawl can be found on page 44 of the Projects Book.*

*This intricate pillow front shows Irish crochet at its best, with flower and leaf motifs on a delicate mesh background.*

in fact to the sewing and knitting bees that many of us enjoy today. Schools quickly sprang up around the centers of lacemaking for the children who needed minding as their mothers worked, so you could credit crochet with the advent of widespread schooling in Ireland, especially for girls. Crochet is still a cottage industry in India, Greece, Italy, and in parts of Asia.

The 19th century saw crochet take off as a fashionable craft when it was used to make accessories and, for the first time in its history, garments. Today, crochet is seen as a modern, stylish handicraft; it is easy to work and portable—perfect for our hectic lifestyles—and the range of designs and projects available to today's crocheter is better than ever.

### THIS TECHNIQUES BOOK

This Techniques Book contains everything you need to know about crochet, from what yarns and hooks are available (see page 8) to how to hold the hook and yarn (page 10).

It is also a comprehensive guide to crochet stitches and will lead you progressively through them, from the simple slip stitch (page 12) to the extra-tall double-triple (page 17). Hints and tips for successful shaping begin on page 19.

The more unusual aspects of crochet are also covered, including delicate filet crochet (page 34) and intricate jacquard designs (page 28).

The accompanying Projects Book is packed with beautiful accessories and fashions for women, babies, and children. You will find cross-references to this Techniques Book with each project, so keep it handy as an easy-to-use guide to all the stitches and techniques required to complete the designs successfully.

*Modern yarns, such as this multicolored fashion yarn, have given crochet a new lease on life. It is quick and easy to work with and gives fantastic results.*

INTRODUCTION

# The basics

You don't need a lot of expensive equipment to crochet—just a crochet hook and a ball of yarn. Learn the techniques by following our step-by-step illustrated instructions, practice with some easy designs (see the Projects Book), and in no time at all, you'll feel confident to tackle any project.

## ABOUT YOUR KIT

In the kit you will find everything you need to get started crocheting… plain and multicolored yarn, E/4 (3.50mm) hook, and materials for your first exciting project, plus extra equipment that will be useful for all your crochet work. Here's exactly what you get:

**1.** Two hanks (one plain, one multicolored) of yarn, enough for the purse or cushion front shown on page 6 in the Projects Book.

**2.** Additional crochet hook in size K/10½ (7.00mm).

**3.** Tapestry needle—thick, with a blunt tip to weave in yarn ends and sew your projects together.

**4.** Beads—12 faceted crystal beads in blue to match the yarn. Use to decorate your bag.

**5.** Lining fabric in a color that blends with the yarn—sufficient to line your purse or cushion front.

**6.** Sewing needle and matching thread to hand sew the lining and attach the beads.

# Hooks and yarns

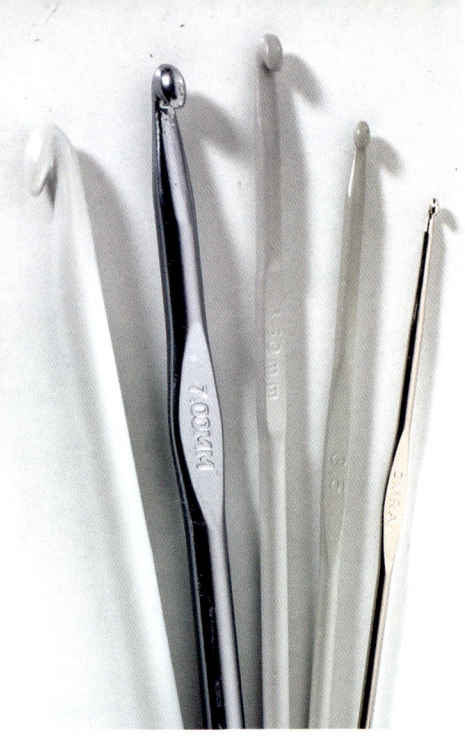

The type and mixture of fibers used in spinning yarn determines its character and texture—whether it is smooth, crepe, bouclé, or metallic. After choosing a yarn, use the simple skill of making stitches with a crochet hook to transform it into a fabulous fabric.

## HOOKS

These simple implements—all you need for working crochet—are graded in size according to the thickness of the yarn being used. Hooks generally fall into one of three categories: steel—for traditional, fine, and delicate work with crochet cotton; aluminum (wood and bamboo are also available)—for standard hand-knitting-weight yarns; and acrylic—for bulky yarns.

There are two different methods used to size hooks—standard U.S. sizing and the European metric system, now widely adopted. The conversion chart (right) shows you how the sizes compare between the two systems and indicates the thickness of yarn compatible with a range of hook sizes. Usually it is important to pair the yarn and its correct-sized hook, but sometimes a much larger or smaller hook is recommended to create a special fabric or effect.

**CROCHET HOOK CONVERSION CHART**

| U.S. | Metric (mm) | Suitable yarns |
|---|---|---|
| **Steel hooks** | | |
| 14 | 0.60 | Traditional fine |
| 12 | 0.75 | crochet cotton |
| 10 | 1.00 | |
| 8 | 1.25 | |
| 7 | 1.50 | |
| 5 | 1.75 | |
| **Aluminum or acrylic hooks** | | |
| B/1 | 2.00 | |
| C/2 | 2.50 | |
| D/3 | 3.25 | 4-ply |
| E/4 | 3.50 | |
| F/5 | 3.75 | |
| G/6 | 4.00 | Worsted and crepe |
| 7 | 4.50 | |
| H/8 | 5.00 | Sport weight |
| I/9 | 5.50 | |
| J/10 | 6.00 | Chunky |
| K/10½ | 7.00 | |
| L/11 | 8.00 | Extra chunky |
| M/13 | 9.00 | |
| N/15 | 10.00 | |

## YARNS

Traditionally, crochet was worked with tiny steel hooks and crochet cotton—smooth and tightly twisted so that the hook did not split the yarn—but even in its thickest form, crochet cotton is still very fine and difficult for beginners to handle.

Today, hand-knitting yarns are frequently used for crochet. They are much thicker than crochet cotton and so much easier to work with. Standard hand-knitting yarns, such as pure wool or a wool-and-acrylic mixture, such as worsted, are suitable for crochet (although lightweight, synthetic fibers, such as acrylic, are preferable for large items). Crepe yarns are ideal to work with because their tight construction prevents the yarn from splitting.

Fashion trends often favor fancy textured yarns, and it is increasingly popular to incorporate these into crochet designs. Often, these extravagant yarns are used as a feature or trim on a more conventional crochet item, but when worked with a large hook in an openwork pattern, they can create very distinctive effects. The fancy texture of the yarn makes it very forgiving of any unevenness in the crochet stitches.

## SUBSTITUTING YARNS

For the best results, it is advisable to use the yarn recommended in the pattern and to work a test swatch beforehand to check your gauge (see Projects Book, page 4).

Substituting the yarn stated in a pattern with another one requires careful attention to check that the yarns are similar enough to obtain a good result, as well as some math to ensure that you have sufficient yarn to complete the project.

The new yarn should be as close as possible to the original. Refer to the ball bands to discover the yardage per ounce (meters per gram) of each yarn. Use a calculator to divide the yards (meters) by the weight of the ball of yarn to find out how many yards (meters) per ounce (gram). Compare the answers—the yarns should be within ten yards (nine meters) of each other to work well.

It is also best to replace a yarn with similar fibers, so substitute wool with wool and cotton with cotton. If you want to substitute a wool with cotton (which, although it has a similar diameter, is much heavier than a wool yarn), then for an accurate estimate, you will need to base your calculation on the total yardage (meterage) of the project rather than each ball of yarn. Multiply the yardage (meterage) per ball of yarn by the total number of balls used, and then work the calculation described here.

HOOKS AND YARNS

# Getting started

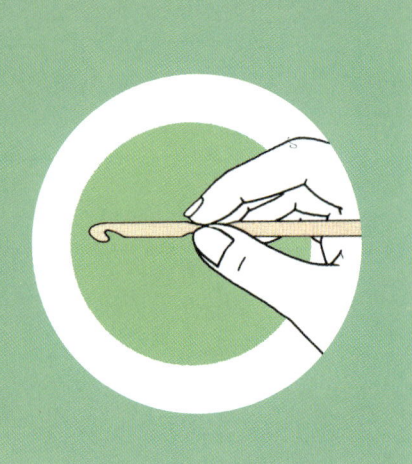

Everyone eventually develops a personal style of crocheting, but before you begin, take some time to practice the following method of holding the hook and controlling the yarn.

## Holding the hook

Hold the hook in your right hand in the same way as a pencil, with the thumb and forefinger over the flat section of the hook.

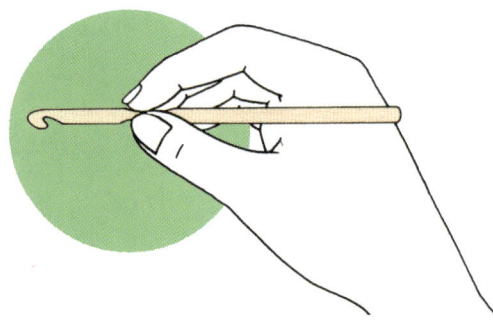

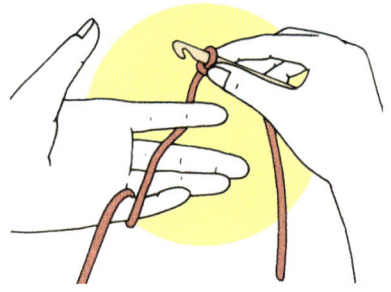

## Controlling the yarn

The left hand holds the work and controls the yarn supply. Once the first loop is on the hook (see "Making a slip loop," right), wind the yarn once around the little finger, take it across the inside of the fingers, and loop it over the index finger. Use the index finger to manipulate the yarn as you work, while the middle finger helps to hold the work.

**Technique Tip** If you are left-handed, prop the book up near a mirror so that you can work from the "mirror image" of the illustrations. However, you will need to read the instructions from the original page. If this proves difficult, you can photocopy the directions and read from these, while looking at the illustrations in the mirror.

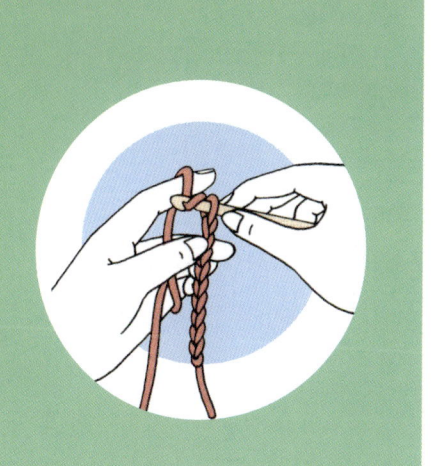

# Foundation chains

All crochet starts with one stitch—a slip loop—on the hook. From the slip loop, a series of chain stitches, called the base or foundation chain, are worked.

## Making a slip loop

Make a slip loop, as shown at right, about 6 in. (15cm) from the cut end of yarn. Insert the crochet hook through the loop, and then gently tighten the knot on the neck of the hook.

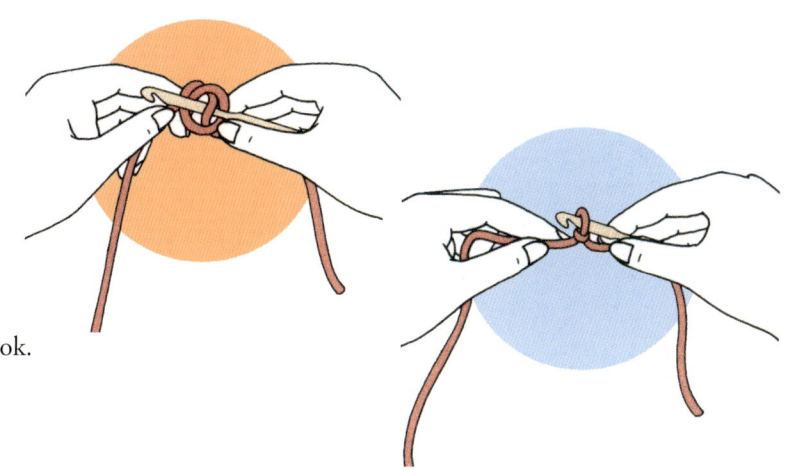

## Making chain stitches (ch)

**1.** Wind the yarn around the hook in a counterclockwise direction, as shown at left.

**2.** Draw the yarn through to form a new loop on the hook. One chain stitch has been worked. Repeat steps 1 and 2 to make the required number of chain stitches, as shown at right.

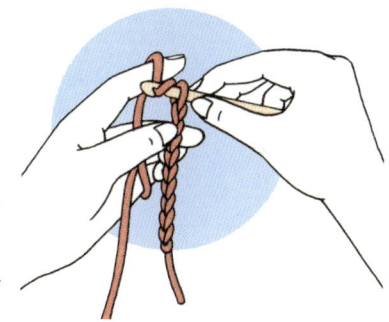

**Technique Tip** To count chains, make sure they are not twisted and that you are looking at the "front," where the chain effect is apparent, as shown in step 2, at right. Then count back from the hook, without counting the loop on the hook.

FOUNDATION CHAINS 11

# Basic stitches

You need to learn only a few crochet techniques in order to produce the basic stitches that vary in height from very short (slip stitch) to very high (double-triple crochet).

## Slip stitch (ss)

This stitch has virtually no depth. It is shown here being worked into a base chain. However, it is usually worked over a fabric made from the other stitches. Slip stitches have three main purposes: to move unobtrusively from one point in the fabric to another; to close a ring when working in rounds; and to join two finished pieces of work together.

**1.** To work into the base chain, insert the hook into the second chain from the hook, wind the yarn around the hook, and draw it through both loops on the hook, as shown at left.

**2.** Continue working into each chain, as shown at right, until the required position is reached.

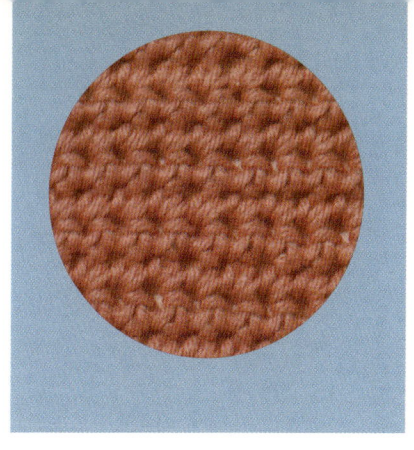

## Single crochet (sc)

This is the shortest crochet stitch that can be repeated throughout to make a fabric. The resulting fabric is usually quite dense. Single crochet is also a popular stitch for working crochet edgings.

**1.** Insert the hook into the second chain from the hook, wind the yarn around the hook, and draw a loop through to make two loops on the hook, as shown below.

**2.** Wind the yarn around the hook and draw it through both loops, as shown below, to complete one single crochet.

**3.** Working into each chain in turn, repeat steps 1 and 2. After the last stitch, turn and make one turning chain before inserting hook into first stitch to start the next row, as shown below.

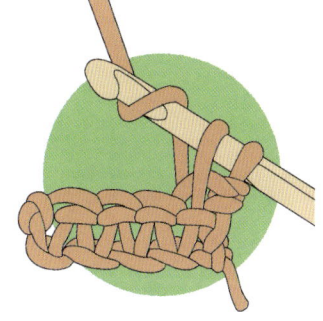

**Technique Tip** Always refer to the pattern you are working from to check the status of the turning chain—in some, the turning chain is counted as the first stitch in the row, while in others, it is disregarded (see page 14, under half-double crochet).

BASIC STITCHES

# Half-double crochet (hdc)

Halfway in height between a single crochet and a double crochet, half-double crochet is another popular fabric stitch.

**1.** Wind the yarn around the hook, insert it into the third chain from the hook, as shown at left, and draw a loop through to make three loops on the hook.

**2.** Wind the yarn around the hook again and draw it through all three loops on the hook, as shown at left, to complete one half-double crochet.

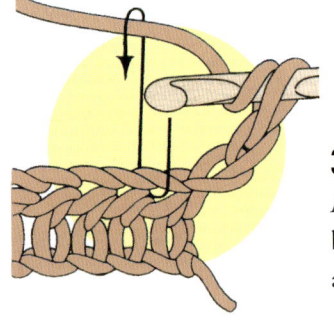

**3.** Working into each chain in turn, repeat steps 1 and 2. After the last stitch, turn and make two turning chains before inserting hook into second stitch to start the next row, as shown at left.

# Double crochet (dc)

Along with single crochet, this is one of the most frequently used fabric stitches. The medium height of double crochet stitches creates a fabric that is both firm and flexible without being too dense.

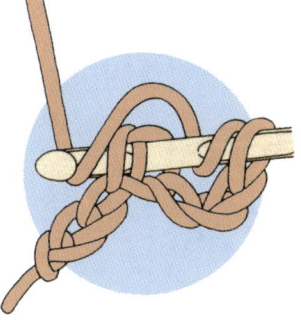

**1.** Wind the yarn around the hook, insert it into the fourth chain from the hook, as shown at left, and draw a loop through to make three loops on the hook.

**2.** Wind the yarn around the hook again and draw it through the first two loops only to make two loops on the hook. Wind the yarn around the hook again and draw it through both loops, as shown at right, to complete one double crochet.

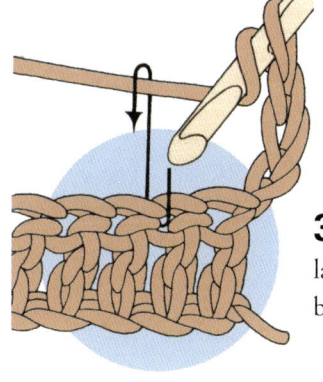

**3.** Working into each chain in turn, repeat steps 1 and 2. After the last stitch, turn and make three turning chains, as shown at left, before inserting hook into second stitch to start the next row.

# Triple crochet (tr)

Both triple and double-triple crochet are variations of double crochet. Winding the yarn round the hook an extra time at the start of each stitch creates extremely tall stitches and a fabric that is loose and open.

**1.** Wind the yarn twice around the hook, insert it into the fifth chain from the hook, as shown at right, and draw a loop through to make four loops on the hook.

**2.** Wind the yarn around the hook again and draw it through the first two loops only, to make three loops on the hook. Wind the yarn around the hook again and draw it through the first two loops only to make two loops on the hook. Wind the yarn round the hook again and draw it through both loops, as shown at left, to complete one triple crochet.

**3.** Working into each chain in turn, repeat steps 1 and 2. After the last stitch, turn and make four turning chains, as shown at right, before inserting hook into second stitch to start the next row.

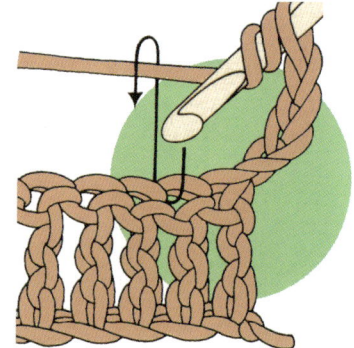

## Double-triple crochet (dtr)

This is the tallest crochet stitch. It is used mainly in decorative openwork patterns and rarely as a fabric, because it is so loose and open.

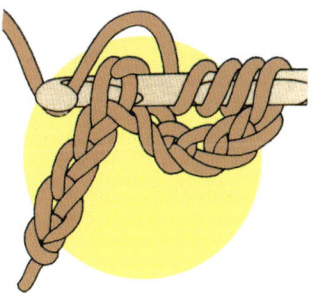

**1.** Wind the yarn three times around the hook, insert it into the sixth chain from the hook, as shown at right, and draw a loop through to make five loops on the hook.

**2.** Wind the yarn around the hook again and draw it through the first two loops only to make four loops on the hook. Now repeat step 2 of triple crochet, as shown at left, to complete one double-triple crochet.

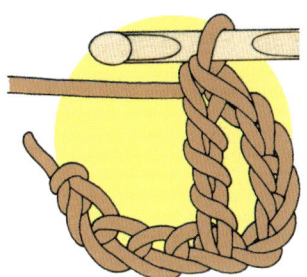

**3.** Working into each chain in turn, repeat steps 1 and 2. After the last stitch, turn and make five turning chains, as shown at right, before inserting hook into the second stitch to start the next row.

**Technique Tip** Beginners can create a project, such as a scarf, quickly and easily simply by working throughout in double-triple crochet, using extra-chunky yarn and the large hook in the kit.

BASIC STITCHES

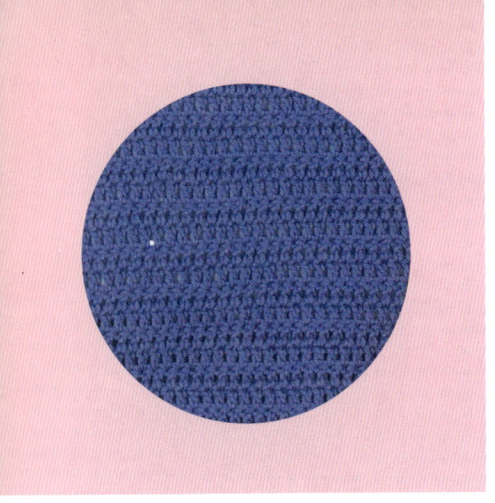

# Making a flat fabric

Most crochet fabrics are worked flat in rows, with the work being turned at the end of each row. As crochet stitches are varying heights (see "Basic Stitches," pages 12–17), each row starts with a "turning chain" that is equivalent in height to the stitch being worked.

## Working in rows

**Turning chain at the start of a fabric**
When working the first row of stitches into the foundation chain, the first stitch is always worked into the 2nd, 3rd, 4th, 5th, or 6th chain from the hook.

The number of "missed" chains depends on the stitch being worked. Afterward, the chain bends upward so that the hook is at the same height as the crochet stitches to be worked.

At the end of the first row, turn the crochet so that you are ready to work again from right to left (or left to right, in the case of left-handers), making the turning chain and another row of stitches on top of those in the previous row.

**Turning chain at the start of rows**
On the second and subsequent rows, work a turning chain, as shown below, to bring the hook up to the height of the stitch to be worked:
1ch = sc; 2ch = hdc; 3ch = dc; 4ch = tr; 5ch = dtr; 5ch = tr tr.

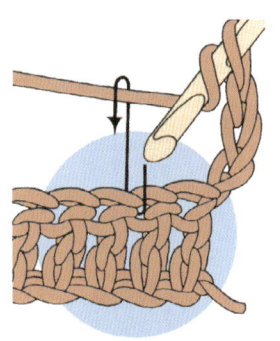

**1.** Work the number of turning chains as directed; then work the first stitch into the top of the second stitch in the previous row, inserting the hook under the two loops forming the chain effect at the top of the stitch.

**2.** Work into each stitch across the row, working the last stitch into the top of the turning chain in the previous row. Turn the work, and you're ready to start another row.

**Fastening off**
To secure the yarn at the end of a piece of work and stop it from unraveling, make one chain and then cut the yarn 2 in. (5cm) away from the hook (or leave a longer end if you want to sew pieces of work together with it). Draw the cut end through the chain and gently tighten the stitch.

# Shaping

To give a crochet garment the required shape, you must increase or decrease stitches at specific points (which will be specified in the pattern). Some crochet-stitch patterns also feature increased or decreased stitches that are part of their design characteristics.

## Single increases

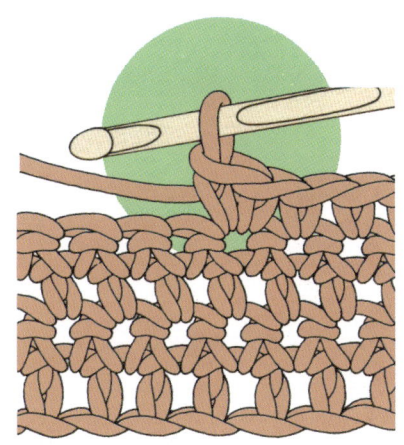

A single increase of one stitch can be made by simply working twice into the same stitch, as shown at left. Although single increases can be made at any point in the row, they are frequently worked at the beginning and end of rows, especially in a garment where this type of increasing is used to shape side seams.

To increase one stitch at the beginning of a row, work the correct number of turning chains; then work two stitches into the next stitch.

To increase one stitch at the end of a row, simply work two stitches into the last stitch.

> **! Technique Tip** Increases can be used to make a triangular motif (see swatch at top of page) for patchwork fabrics. Start off with two or three stitches and increase at each end of every row until the motif is the required size.

# Multiple increases

If more than two stitches need to be added at the edge of a fabric, additional chains are made. This method is frequently used for adding sleeves to the body of a garment as you crochet.

**Increasing at the beginning of a row**

Work chains corresponding in number to the extra stitches required plus a turning chain, as shown at right (so if you are working in single crochet and need four extra stitches, work five chains in total). Work one single crochet into the second chain from the hook, then into each of the next three chains and continue across the row as usual.

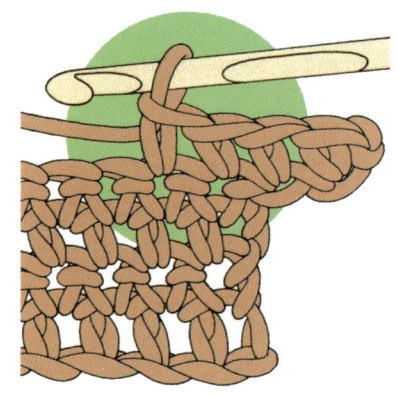

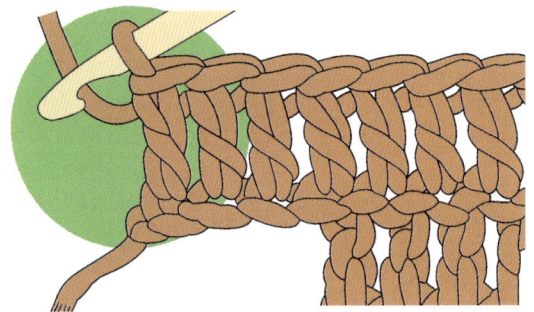

**Increasing at the end of the row**

To increase four stitches at the end of the row, remove the hook from the working loop temporarily. Using another length of the same yarn, make four chains and join with a slip stitch to the last stitch in the previous row. Fasten off. Now, return to the working loop and work four new stitches into the extra chains.

> **! Technique Tip** Multiple increases at both edges of the work must be worked as above—not at the start of two consecutive rows. If worked on consecutive rows, the height of the crochet stitches would make the increases appear unbalanced.

# Single decreases

The most popular method of decreasing involves narrowing the fabric by working two stitches together as one. This technique can be used with any of the basic stitches and often appears as a series of paired decreases at the beginning and end of rows.

### Decreasing 1 stitch in single crochet (sc2tog) or half-double crochet (hdc2tog)

Insert the hook into each of the two stitches to be decreased and draw a loop through, so making three loops on the hook, as shown at right. Wind the yarn around the hook and draw it through all three loops to complete the decrease.

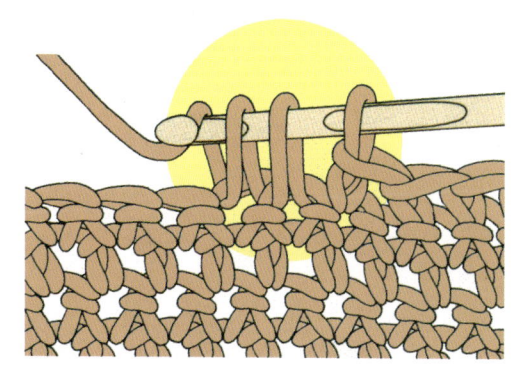

### Alternative decreasing 1 stitch in half-double crochet (hdc2tog)

This is another method of working two half-double crochet together. (Wind the yarn around the hook, insert it into the next stitch, and draw a loop through) twice, so making five loops on the hook. Wind the yarn round the hook and draw it through all five loops to complete the decrease.

### Decreasing 1 stitch in double crochet (dc2tog)

Work as follows into each of the two stitches to be decreased: (Wind the yarn around the hook, insert it into the next stitch and draw a loop through, wind the yarn around the hook and draw it through the first two loops), so making three loops on the hook. Wind the yarn around the hook, as shown at right, and draw it through all three loops to complete the decrease.

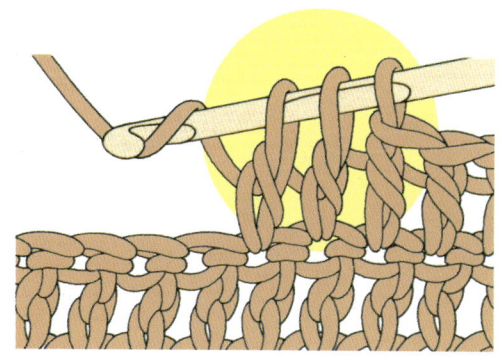

SHAPING  21

# Double decreases

Sometimes it is necessary to decrease three stitches together instead of two. Again the technique applies to all the basic stitches and can be used at any point in the row—beginning, middle, or end.

**Decreasing 2 stitches in single crochet (sc3tog) or half-double crochet (hdc3tog)**

Insert the hook into the first stitch to be decreased and draw a loop through, skip the next stitch, then insert hook into last stitch to be decreased, as shown at right, and draw a loop through, so making three loops on the hook. Wind the yarn around the hook and draw it through all three loops to complete the decrease.

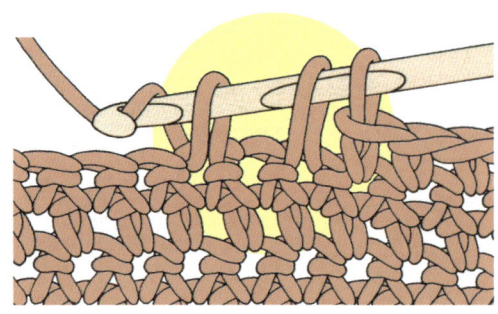

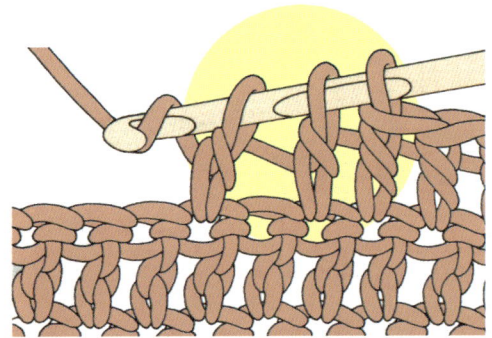

**Decreasing 2 stitches in double crochet (dc3tog)**

\* Wind the yarn around the hook, insert it into the next stitch and draw a loop through, wind the yarn round the hook and draw it through the first two loops \*, skip the next stitch, repeat from \* to \* so making three loops on the hook. Wind the yarn around the hook, as shown at left, and draw it through all three loops to complete the decrease.

!**Technique Tip** The methods of decreasing shown here can be adapted for any of the taller stitches, such as triple and double-triple crochet. Simply work the loops off the hook as demonstrated in the diagrams.

# Multiple decreases

Another form of decreasing, also known as "step decreasing," leaves a number of stitches unworked at the beginning and end of rows. This method is often used at the start of the underarm shaping on a garment.

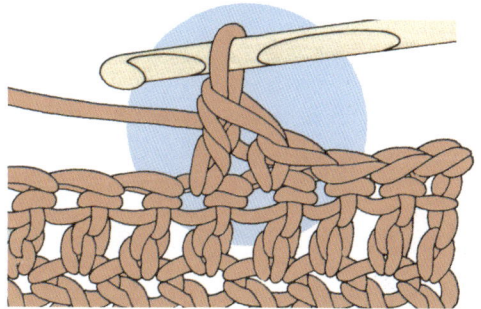

**1.** At the beginning of a row, slip stitch into each of the stitches to be decreased, work one single crochet into the next stitch, as shown at left, and complete the row in pattern as instructed.

**2.** At the end of the row, to avoid an abrupt change in stitch heights, leave unworked the number of stitches to be decreased, slip stitch into the next stitch, turn, and work one chain. Skip the slip stitch, work one single crochet into the next stitch, and complete the row in pattern, as shown at right.

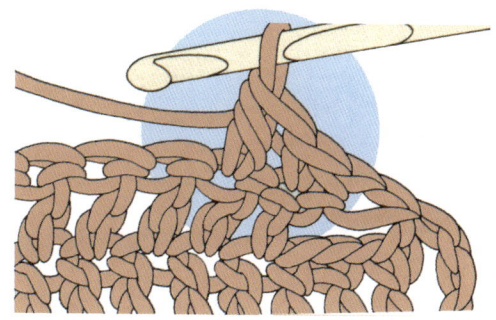

**Technique Tip** The single crochet stitch worked after the multiple decreases here makes a smooth transition to the taller stitches in the fabric, but it is not always included in pattern instructions.

# Working in rounds

Crochet motifs are worked in rounds, starting from the center and working outward, always from the right side. Gradual increasing on each round makes the circle grow in size and ensures that it will lie flat.

Although a motif starts off as a circle, it can be developed into a number of other shapes, including squares and octagons. Practice your crochet techniques by working the different styles of motifs shown on the opposite page.

**1.** To form a starting circle, make three or more chains (the exact number will be specified in the pattern) and join them into a ring by inserting the hook into the first chain and working a slip stitch, as shown above.

**2.** At the start of each round, work a number of chain equivalent to the height of the stitch being worked (see "Turning chain," page 18); then work all the stitches in the first round into the center of the chain ring, as shown above.

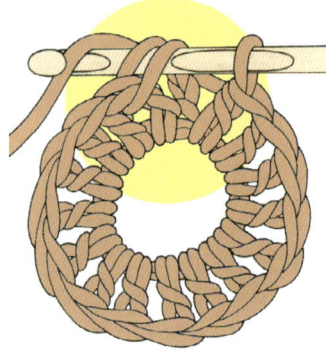

**3.** At the end of the round, join the stitches into a circle by inserting the hook into the top of the starting chain, as shown above, and working a slip stitch. On the second and subsequent rounds, after working the starting chain, insert the hook under the top two loops of the stitches in the previous round unless instructed otherwise.

### Circular motif

Concentric rounds to form a circular motif must be worked with enough increases to keep the edges from curling. The general formula is to increase every round by the number of stitches you started with.

Make 6ch, join with a ss into first ch to form a ring.
**1st round** 3ch, 11dc into ring, join with a ss into top of 3ch. 12 sts.
**2nd round** 3ch, 1dc into ss, 2dc into each dc, join with a ss into 3rd of 3ch. 24 sts.
**3rd round** 3ch, 2dc into next dc, (1dc into next dc, 2dc into next dc) 11 times, join with a ss into 3rd of 3ch. 36 sts.

Continue to increase 12 sts in this way on every round (in every 3rd st on next round, then every 4th st on following round, and so on) until the circle is the required size.

### Square motif

One of the most popular crochet motifs, this one starts off as a circle but ends up as a square.

Make 6ch, join with a ss into first ch to form a ring.
**1st round** 3ch, 2dc into ring 1ch, (3dc into ring, 1ch) 3 times, join with a ss into 3rd of 3ch. 12 sts.
**2nd round** 3ch, 1dc into each of next 2 sts, * (2dc, 1ch, 2dc) into ch sp, 1dc into each of next 3 sts, rep from * to last ch sp, (2dc, 1ch, 2dc) into last ch sp, join with a ss into 3rd of 3ch. 28 sts.
**3rd round** 3ch, 1dc into each of next 4 sts, * (2dc, 1ch, 2dc) into ch sp, 1dc into each of next 7 sts, rep from * to last ch sp, (2dc, 1ch, 1dc) into last ch sp, join with a ss into 3rd of 3ch. 44 sts.

Continue evenly along each side, working (2dc, 1ch, 2dc) into ch sp at each corner and increasing 16 sts in total on every round.

### Octagonal motif

This eight-sided motif has two increases at each angle, instead of four, to keep it flat.

Make 4ch, join with a ss into first ch to form a ring.
**1st round** 2ch, 1hdc into ring, 1ch, (2hdc into ring, 1ch) 7 times, join with a ss into 3rd of 3ch. 16 sts.
**2nd round** 2ch, 1hdc into next st, *(1hdc, 1ch, 1hdc) into ch sp, 1hdc into each of next 2 sts, rep from * to last ch sp, (1hdc, 1ch, 1hdc) into last ch sp, join with a ss into 3rd of 3ch. 32 sts.
**3rd round** 2ch, 1hdc into each of next 3 sts, *(1hdc, 1ch, 1hdc) into ch sp, 1hdc into each of next 4 sts, rep from * to last ch sp, (1hdc, 1ch, 1hdc) into last ch sp, join with a ss into 3rd of 3ch. 48 sts.

Continue evenly along each side, working (1hdc, 1ch, 1hdc) at each angle and increasing 16 sts in total on every round.

# Color effects

One of the easiest ways to create a colorful effect, as well as being an economical method of using up remnants of yarn in the same thickness, is with simple stripes—both horizontal and vertical. Before starting any color projects, first practice the techniques involved in changing colors.

## Joining in new yarn at the end of a row

When working in a single color or horizontal stripes, it is usual to join in the new yarn at the end of a row (always change to a new ball of yarn or color before you complete the last stitch with the old yarn or color) so that it is ready to work the turning chain at the start of the new row. This method also secures and neatens the yarn ends at the same time.

The same methods are useful for a variety of color work, including stripes and Jacquard, as well as being essential for most one-color projects.

**1.** When working the last stitch of the row below the color change, just before working the last stage of the final stitch (shown here in single crochet), drop the old yarn and pick up the new yarn or color, winding it over the hook. Draw the new color through to complete the stitch, as shown at right.

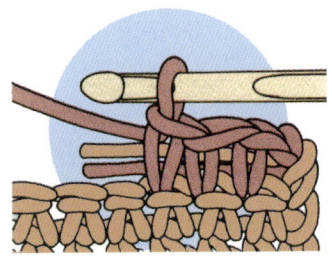

**2.** Cut the old color to 2 in. (5cm), make one chain, and turn. Lay both short yarn ends over the previous row and work over them for four or five stitches, as shown at left. Carefully trim off any remaining yarn ends close to the fabric.

## Changing color in the middle of a row

Joining in yarn by this method eliminates the need to weave in the yarn ends with a tapestry needle when the project is complete.

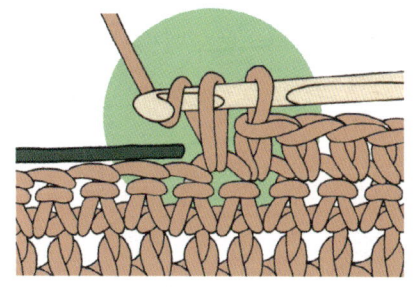

**1.** A few stitches before you need it, lay the end of the new yarn color over the row below, as shown at right. Continue to work with the first color, covering the new end of yarn.

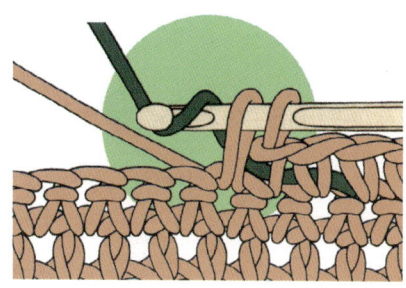

**2.** Work the first color to the final two loops of the last stitch, as shown above; then draw the new color through these last two loops to complete the stitch, also shown above.

## Working stripes

**Horizontal stripes**
Work an even number of rows in each stripe to carry the color not in use up the side of the work until you need it again. For irregular stripes, as shown above, join in new colors where required, following steps 1 and 2 of "Joining in new yarn at the end of a row," left.

**Narrow vertical stripes**
If you stick to two colors and a maximum of four or five stitches in each stripe, you can loosely strand the color not in use across the back of the work (see "Carrying yarn across back of work," page 28). Remember that the finished fabric will be double the thickness because of the stranded yarns.

**Wide vertical stripes**
When the distance between stripes is more than four or five stitches, use a small, separate ball of yarn for each stripe. When changing color, remember to introduce the new color to complete the last part of the final stitch in the old color, as shown in steps 1 and 2 of "Changing color in the middle of a row," above.

COLOR EFFECTS 27

## Jacquard designs

Multicolored effects, such as allover patterned fabrics or individual motifs on a plain background, are popular in crochet. Simple designs, such as geometrics, work best because it can be difficult to achieve fine details. Depending on the situation, there are three methods of working colored (or Jacquard) patterns. Always make the color change by completing the final stitch in the old color with the new yarn (see "Changing color in the middle of a row," page 27).

## Carrying yarn across back of work

In the photo at left, the yarn not in use is stranded across the wrong side of the work. If you need to carry it over more than three stitches, weave it in with every other stitch as shown in the diagrams, below. To change colors on a right-side row, work the first color to the final two loops, drop the first color back and to the left of the new color, and then complete the stitch with the new color, as shown on page 26. To change colors on wrong-side row, work as before, but drop the old color forward and to the right of the new color.

## Weaving in yarn

Yarn carried over more than three stitches should be woven in to prevent the strands from pulling. For an even tension, without puckering, take care not to apply tension to the yarn being carried.

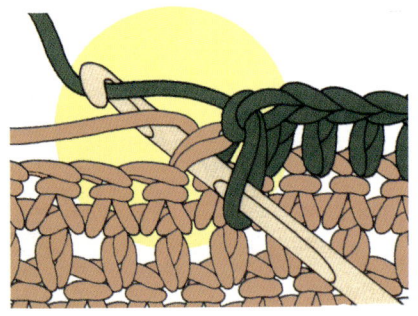

**1.** On a right-side row, insert the hook into the stitch, then under the carried yarn at the back of the work, catch working yarn with the hook, as shown at left, draw through a loop, and complete the stitch.

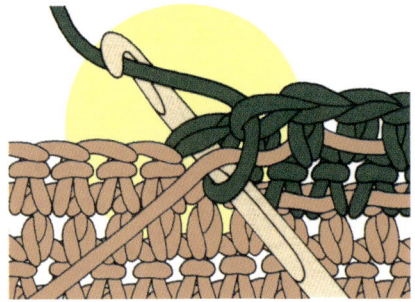

**2.** On a wrong-side row, insert hook under the carried yarn, then into the stitch, catch working yarn with the hook, as shown above, draw through a loop, and complete the stitch.

# Working from a color chart

Color patterns, especially motifs, are often given in chart form. At right is a graph where each square equals a stitch and each line equals a row. Usually, blank squares represent the main color, and the pattern is depicted with colored squares or symbols or a mixture of both. To follow a chart, start work at the bottom right-hand corner and read from right to left for right-side rows and left to right for wrong-side rows.

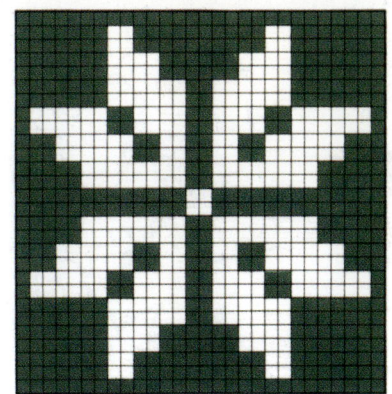

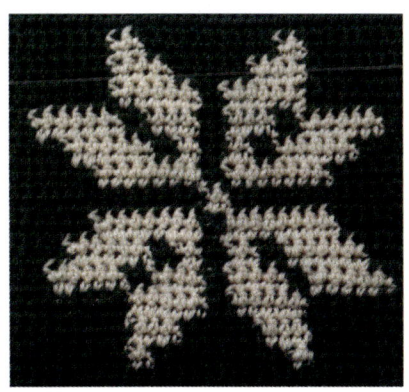

For the motif shown at left, the color changes have been managed by cutting and weaving in the yarn ends. This is practical when yarn must be carried a long way, when colors are changed at the end of a row, or when the pattern is an inset motif. It also means that the fabric is reversible.

To discontinue a color, work it to the final two loops of the last stitch; then draw through a loop in the new color. Cut off the first color, leaving a 6-in. (15-cm) end. When the work is complete, weave the yarn end through several stitches in a matching color and trim the remainder.

**Technique Tip** Use the tapestry needle in your kit to weave in yarn ends, as well as for sewing projects together. Its large eye is perfect for thicker yarns, and the blunt tip will not split the yarn.

JACQUARD DESIGNS

# Stitch variations

Interesting textured fabrics can be created in crochet, even using just plain yarn. Once you have mastered the basic stitches, it is easy to vary them by inserting the hook into different parts of the fabric and manipulating the hook to form an unusual effect.

## Raised stitches

Throw any crochet stitch into relief by working around the stem of the stitch one or more rows below. You can create this effect from either the front or back of the work, as shown in the samples below and above right.

### Raised double crochet at the back

Wind the yarn around the hook. Insert the hook from the front and then from right to left around the stem of the stitch below, as shown at right. Wind the yarn round the hook again, draw it through the stitch below (three loops on hook), and complete the double crochet in the usual way.

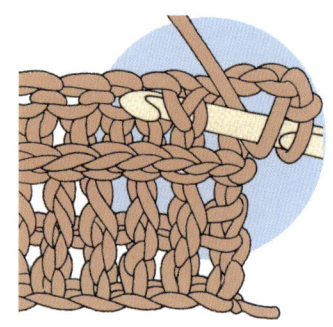

**! Technique Tip** If you are making a raised stitch more than one row below, you will have to work a taller stitch, such as a triple crochet.

## Raised double crochet at the front

Wind the yarn around the hook. Insert the hook from the back and then from right to left around the stem of the stitch below, as shown at right. Wind the yarn round the hook again, draw it through the stitch below (three loops on hook), and complete the double crochet.

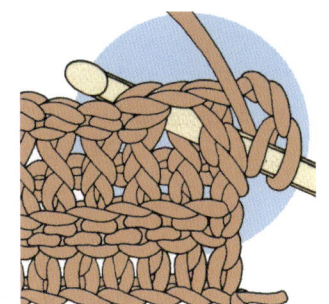

> **Technique Tip** You can also work the "ribbed" effect described below directly onto the edge of a garment, rather than sewing it on.

## Ridged effects

You can make ridges in crochet (they look like knitted ribbing but lack its elasticity) by continuously working under the back loop or the front loop of the stitch below. This ridged effect is usually used to form the "ribbing" on crochet garments.

In this ridge-stitch ribbing, the ridges are formed horizontally, then turned sideways for ribbing.

Make any number of chain stitches that will form the required length of the ribbing.
**1st row** 1sc into 2nd ch from hook, 1sc into each ch to end, turn.
**2nd row** 1ch, 1sc into back loop only of each st to end, turn.
Rep 2nd row to form the patt.

When the ribbing is long enough for the garment edge, fasten off and work as directed in the instructions along one side of the ridge pattern.

## Loops

These shaggy loops are worked over the fingers and appear on the right side of the fabric, while the reverse is a firm single-crochet background fabric. Use this stitch to make a novelty fabric for home furnishings or for details, such as looped edgings on a garment.

To form loops over the fingers, first work a foundation row of single crochet in the desired length and turn. Work 1ch, * insert hook into next st, swing 3rd and 4th fingers of left hand forward under yarn, then back against the yarn so that a 1-in. (2.5-cm)-long loop is formed over these fingers, as shown below, right. Draw a loop through the st, pulling it over the top of the 3rd finger, yrh and draw through two loops, slip fingers out of the loop, rep from * to end of row. On the following (wrong-side) row, work in single crochet.

**Technique Tip** Loops can be cut for a shaggy effect. Slide a ruler or strip of stiff cardboard through a row of loops and cut along the outer edge.

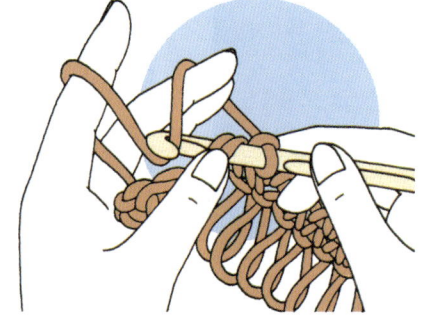

## Clusters

A cluster is a number of stitches (usually three to five) all worked into the same place, then drawn together at the top with one loop. Depending on how many stitches are in the group, the results may be relatively flat (see photograph of soft clusters, left ) or very chunky (as in Bobble stitch, page 33). An allover cluster pattern makes a warm, bulky fabric. Used individually or as a single row, clusters look attractive as an accent or trim.

## Soft clusters (in dc)

This fairly flat-stitch grouping looks the same on both sides of the fabric.

Make a multiple of 2ch, plus 4 extra.
**1st row** Into 4th ch from hook, work (yrh, insert hook into ch and draw through a loop, yrh and draw through 2 loops) 3 times into same ch, yrh and draw through all 4 loops—1 cluster formed, *1ch, skip 1ch, 1 cluster into next ch, rep from * to end, turn.
**2nd row** 3ch, *1 cluster into ch-sp between clusters of previous row, rep from * ending with 1 cluster into 3rd of 3ch, turn.
Rep 2nd row to form patt.

## Bobble stitch

A solid, three-dimensional pattern that requires plenty of yarn.

Make a multiple of 3ch, plus 1 extra.
**1st row** 1sc into 2nd ch from hook, 1sc into each ch to end, turn.
**2nd row** 1ch, work (yrh, insert hook into next st and draw through a loop, yrh and draw through 2 loops) 5 times into same st, yrh and draw through all 6 loops—1 bobble formed, *1sc into each of next 2 sts, 1 bobble into next st, rep from * to end, turn.
**3rd row** 1ch, 1sc into each st to end, turn.
**4th row** 1ch, *1sc into each of next 2 sts, 1 bobble into next st, rep from * to last st, 1sc into last st, turn.
**5th row** As 3rd row.
**6th row** 1ch, 1sc into next st, *1 bobble into next st, 1sc into each of next 2 sts, rep from * to end.
**7th row** As 3rd row.
Rep 2nd to 7th rows to form patt.

> **! Technique Tip** In general, clusters look best in heavy- or medium-weight yarns. When working either a cluster or a bobble, keep the yarn tension fairly loose so that it will be easier to draw the final loop through the top one.

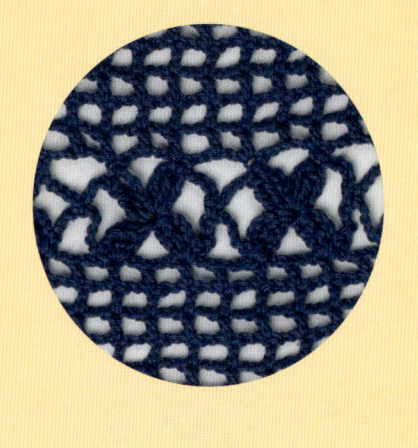

# Filet crochet

This form of crochet consists of a regular square mesh of stitches comprising individual double crochet separated by chains. By filling in chain spaces with double crochet, they become blocks. Depending on the arrangement of blocks and spaces, a variety of designs, including floral motifs, geometric patterns, and lettering, can be created.

Traditionally, filet crochet was worked in fine cotton thread, using a tiny steel hook. It was used to make decorative edgings for household linens or lacy table mats and accessories, such as collars and cuffs, that our ancestors loved. Filet crochet is popular today for its openwork appearance, especially for summer sweaters and tops worked in regular cotton yarn. However, it is just as effective in thicker hand-knitting yarns and larger hooks for a wide range of fashionable garments.

## Basic grid background

Usually, a filet-crochet background consists of single double-crochet stitches separated by two chains, as shown at left. Depending on personal tension, the number of chains between stitches may need to be adjusted to maintain the square proportions of the blocks and spaces.

Make a multiple of 3 chains plus 8 extra chains.
**1st row** (RS) 1dc into 8th ch from hook (7 missed ch count as 2ch sp at the start of the row), *2ch, miss 2ch, 1dc into next ch, rep from * to end.
**2nd row** 5ch (counts as first dc and 2ch), miss first dc and sp, 1dc into next dc, *2ch, miss next sp, 1dc into next dc, rep from * ending with last dc into 5th of first 7ch.
Repeat 2nd row throughout, noting that subsequent last dc are worked into 3rd of first 5ch.

# Using charts for filet-crochet designs

Row-by-row instructions for filet-crochet designs can occasionally be lengthy and repetitive, so it is sometimes easier to work from a chart. Since charts are so visual, you can see the complete pattern—or a whole repeat of it—at once, making it easy to check the way your work is progressing.

Filet crochet charts are slightly different from other crochet charts, as they take the form of a grid of solid squares (blocks, filled in with two double crochet stitches) and open squares (spaces, two double-crochet stitches separated by two chains).

The key and abbreviations tell you how to work the blocks and spaces. The chart is read in the usual way, from the bottom to the top, right-side rows from right to left and wrong-side rows from left to right.

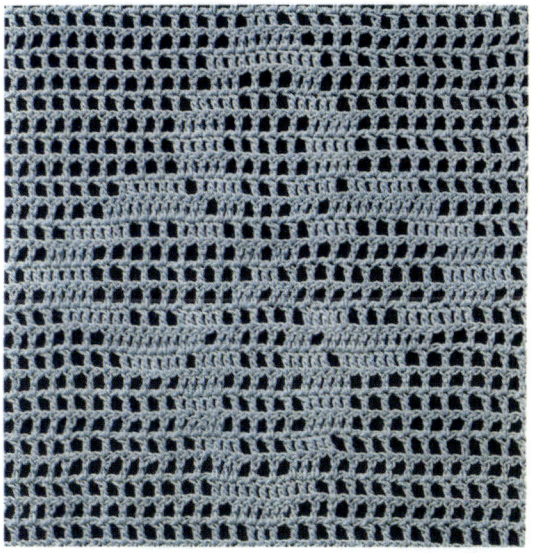

*This floral motif, worked from the chart at left, can be used as an individual motif or an allover repeat.*

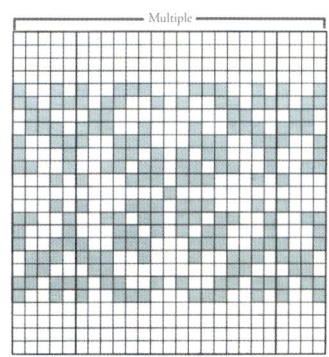

## Key:

◻ = 1 space (1dc, 2ch and skip next sp on 2dc block)

▪ = 1 block (1dc, then 1dc into each of next 2dc or into 2ch sp)

*The flower in this pattern, worked from the above chart, can be repeated to form an attractive border design, as shown in the photo at left.*

FILET CROCHET

# Shaping filet crochet

The decorative quality of many filet-crochet edgings is enhanced by a serrated effect formed by increasing and decreasing blocks and spaces. The principles of shaping filet crochet are the same whether you are making an edging or a garment.

## Increasing a space at the start of a row

Make seven chains to form the additional space, as shown at right; then work one double crochet into the first double crochet of the row—this is the first stitch that you would normally miss. Continue in charted pattern.

## Decreasing a space at the start of a row

Miss the first block or space by slip stitching into each of the first three stitches and then into next double crochet, work three chains (for first double crochet) or five chains (for first double crochet and two-chain space). Continue in charted pattern.

## Decreasing a space at the end of a row

Work pattern to the last block or space in the row (the one formed by the turning chain); then simply turn the work and start the next row. The resulting space is triangular, as shown at right, rather than square.

## Variations on mesh backgrounds

A basic mesh background, as shown on page 34, can be adapted by overlaying it with chain stitches or weaving it with strands of yarn to produce sturdy and colorful plaids, suitable for outerwear, rugs, or place mats.

## Chain overlays

An easy and effective way to create a crocheted stripe.

To work the overlay chains, use two strands of yarn to make a slip knot. With right side of mesh facing you and the yarn held behind the work, draw a loop through the first space in the lower-right corner, insert hook in space directly above it, draw a loop through the space and the loop on the hook. Continue working vertically in this way to the top of the mesh; then begin again at the bottom. Change colors as desired.

## Woven overlays

The woven strands can be yarn, ribbon, or fabric strips and can be worked into the background in any direction.

To weave the overlay, use three strands of yarn threaded into a tapestry needle. Lace the yarns vertically under and over the chain bars, as shown at left, filling alternate spaces on each row. The yarn should be pulled firmly, so that no loops remain, yet not so tightly that the mesh may pucker.

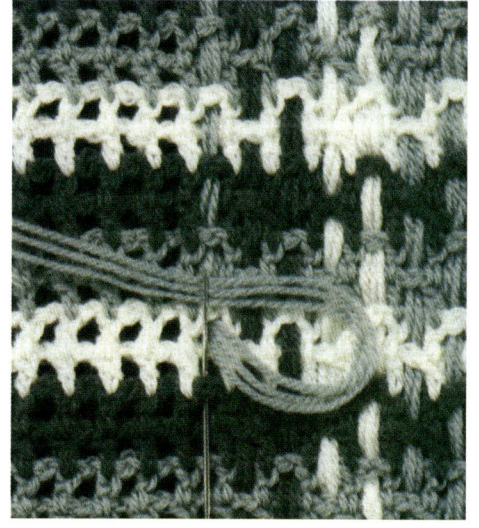

> **❗ Technique Tip**  Maintain an even tension when forming the chains, or the background will be pulled out of shape.

FILET CROCHET

# Charted stitches

Crochet charts show the whole of the pattern in advance, telling you which stitches to make and where to place them. Because a chart looks just like the finished work, it's easy to see where you are at any time—even in the middle of a very complicated pattern. It is especially suited to working in the round.

## Shorthand symbols

Here you can see the crochet symbols and their meanings. Usually, no more than a few symbols are used in a pattern, so you need to remember only those you are using.

Crochet symbols are used in many countries, but they are not necessarily standardized; those shown here are typical but not universal. Sometimes a different picture might have more meaning for you, or you might need a symbol that is not shown here. In either case, you can invent your own symbol.

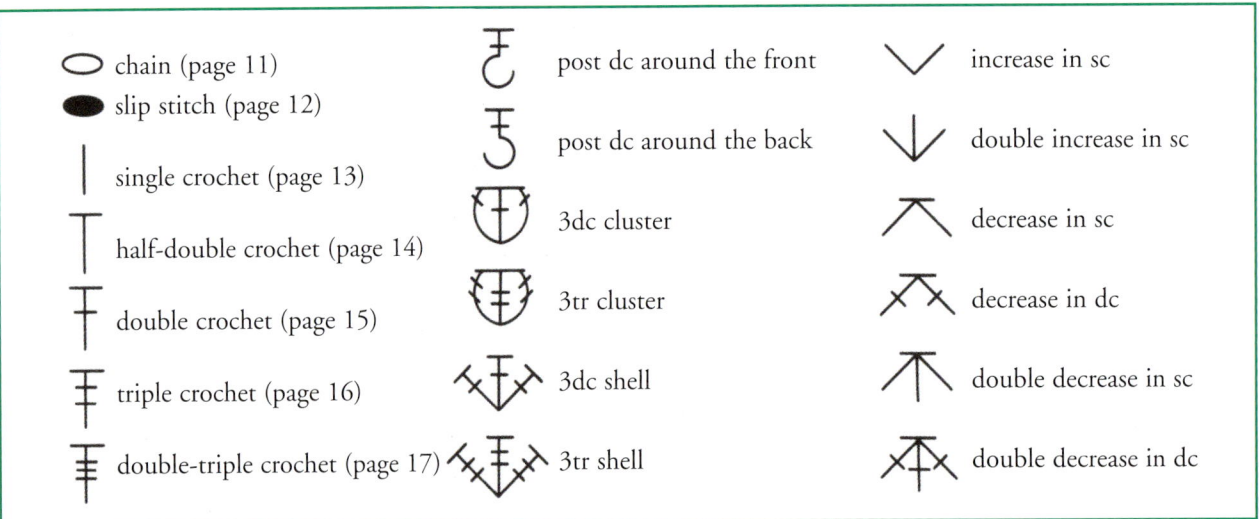